POST CARD

FOR CORRESPONDENCE

FOR ADDRESS ONLY

Message: You're my Angel Mom. Let's look at these together. (You can read them before I come!) Love you always & forever, Nancy

"Mom"
To: Marylou Van Kuren
From: Nancy VK Braun

1

Angel Kisses

Published in Nashville, Tennessee, by Thomas Nelson®, Inc.
Thomas Nelson is a registered trademark of Thomas Nelson®, Inc.

Thomas Nelson, Inc. titles may be purchased in bulk for educational, business,
fund-raising, or sales promotional use. For information, please e-mail SpecialMarkets@ThomasNelson.com.

Thomas Nelson has made every effort to trace the ownership of all quotes in this book. In the event of any question that may arise
from the use of any quote, we regret any error made and will be pleased to make the necessary correction in the future editions of this book.
We sincerely appreciate Rev. David L. Griffith (www.palletmastersworkshop.com)
for allowing us to use his quote, The Difference Between Strength and Courage, © 1997.

Unless otherwise noted, all Scripture references are from *New International Version*
© 1984 by the International Bible Society. Used by permission of Zondervan Bible Publishers.

Other Scripture references are taken from *New King James Version* (NKJV) ©1979, 1980, 1982, 1992, Thomas Nelson, Inc.;
King James Version (KJV); *New Century Version*® (NCV). Copyright © 1987, 1988, 1991 by Thomas Nelson, Inc. All rights reserved;
The Message (MSG) © 1993. Used by permission of NavPress Publishing Group.; *New Living Translation* (NLT) © 1996.
Used by permission of Tyndale House Publishers, Inc., Wheaton, Ill. All rights reserved.

Designed by Lisa Jane with the assistance of Greg Jackson, Thinkpen Design, Inc.
Project Manager: Lisa Stilwell

ISBN-10: 1-4041-8715-4
ISBN-13: 978-1-4041-8715-3

Printed and bound in China

www.thomasnelson.com

08 09 10 11 12—6 5 4 3 2 1

angel kisses

A book of comfort and joy...

FEATURING THE ARTWORK OF

Lisa Jane

I will turn their mourning into gladness;
I will give them comfort and joy instead
of sorrow," declares the Lord.

JEREMIAH 32:13

This book was divinely inspired, and I am honored to be the conduit of it. It is a loving gift from the Father Almighty to His hurting children so that they may have a small glimpse of heaven on earth, and a taste of His enormous love and grace. The quotes, Scriptures, and angelic artwork in this book have had an uplifting effect on my spirit and have aided my healing through painful times. My wish for you is, as you journey through life and the challenges it holds, that you will be able to receive comfort and joy from this collection.

How precious is Your loving kindness, O God!
Therefore the children of men put their trust
under the shadow of your wings.

PSALM 36:7 NKJV

HUGS AND ANGEL KISSES TO YOU!

Lisa Jane

*S*criptures and inspirational quotes soothe my heart and comfort my soul as though it were being kissed by angels.

Lisa Jane

*A*ll that happens to us, good and bad,
presents great possibilities for emotional and
spiritual growth. You and I have
free will. We can pick and choose what
better serves our happiness. This is your
one and only short and precious life.
It could end at any time. This present
moment is really all the time we have
to decide to follow God and live in His light.

NAOMI JUDD, *THE TRANSPARENT LIFE*

*H*e will cover you with His feathers,
and under his wings you
can hide. His truth will be your
shield and protection.

PSALM 91:4 NCV

I know God will not
give me anything I can't handle.
I just wish he didn't trust me so much.

MOTHER TERESA

9

*T*rust in the LORD, and do good;
Dwell in the land, and feed on His faithfulness.
Delight yourself also in the LORD,
And He shall give you the desires of your heart.

PSALM 37:3–4 NKJV

*N*ow the alternative to despair is courage.
And human life can be viewed as a
continuous struggle between these two
options. Courage is the capacity to affirm
one's life in spite of the elements
which threaten it. The fact that courage
usually predominates over despair in itself
tells us something important about life.
It tells you that the forces that affirm
life are stronger than those that negate it.

PAUL E. PFUETZE

You can never do a kindness too soon because
you never know how soon will be too late.

*I*n the giving it
becomes clear that we are
chosen, blessed, and broken not
simply for our own sakes, but so that all
we are about, all that we live, finds its final
significance in its being lived for others."

HENRI NOUWEN

*T*he glory of friendship is not in the
outstretched hand, nor the kindly smile,
or the joy of companionship;
it is in the spiritual inspiration that comes to
one when he discovers that someone else
believes in him and is willing to trust him.

RALPH WALDO EMERSON

*A*nd we know that all things work together for good
to those who love God, to those who are the
called according to His purpose.

ROMANS 8:28 NKJV

*L*et your hopes, not your hurts, shape your future.

ROBERT H. SCHULLER

*T*hrough the LORD's mercies we are not consumed,
Because His compassions fail not.

LAMENTATIONS 3:22–24

*T*here are only two lasting bequests we
can hope to give our children.
One is roots; the other, wings.

HOODING CARTER

The light in children's eyes is the reflection
of heaven peeking through.

KAREN GOLDMAN

Be full of joy in the LORD always.
I will say again, be full of joy.

PHILIPPIANS 4:4 NCV

LORD, tell me your ways. Show me how to live.
Guide me in your truth, and teach me, my God, my Savior.
I trust you all day long. LORD, remember your mercy
and love that you have shown since long ago.

PSALM 25:4–6 NCV

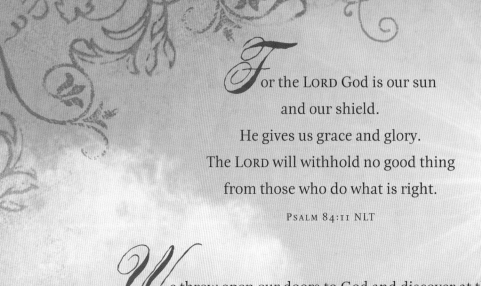

For the LORD God is our sun
and our shield.
He gives us grace and glory.
The LORD will withhold no good thing
from those who do what is right.

PSALM 84:11 NLT

We throw open our doors to God and discover at the same moment
that he has already thrown open his door to us.
We find ourselves standing where we always hoped we might stand—
out in the wide open spaces of God's grace and glory,
standing tall and shouting our praise.

ROMANS 5:2 MSG

Those who go to God Most High for safety
will be protected by the Almighty.
I will say to the LORD,
"You are my place of safety and protection.
You are my God and I trust you."

PSALM 91:1–2 NCV

Lisa Jane

20

I know what I am planning for you," says the LORD. "I have good plans
for you, not plans to hurt you. I will give you hope and a good future.
Then you will call my name. You will come to me and pray to me,
and I will listen to you. You will search for me. And when
you search for me with all your heart, you will find me!"

JEREMIAH 29:11–13 NCV

A few days before my son Dustin's second birthday, as we were all getting ready for his party, I went to the studio next to my house to get my camera. As I put my hand on the door to open it, a sense of dread came over me, chilling me all the way to the pit of my stomach and threatening to ruin what I hoped would be a wonderful day. My mother's instinct told me that something was amiss with my children, and I ran to check on them. But they were all fine, and I saw that the gate to the pond on our property was securely closed. Nonetheless, as I approached the studio door a second time, I once again felt overcome with an insistent, sick feeling.

I started praying. I prayed for protection for my children; I asked God to send extra guardian angels to surround my property. Blessedly, I felt the heavy sense of dread lift and in its place a peace and assurance that God was in control. Slightly relieved, I had picked up my camera and was closing the door when I heard the screaming.

Dustin came stumbling through the gate, soaking wet and covered with pond lilies. He was hysterical, and by the time I reached him, so was I. I held him close and tried to calm him as I brought him inside. After some cuddling and a warm bath, I took Dustin out to sit by the pond, so I could pray and try to figure out what had just occurred.

I sat at the water's edge, thanked God for sparing my son, and asked Him to show me what had happened. As I waited for His answer, I saw a vision of Dustin trying to climb up the rocks on the side of the pond and slipping down into the water; his diaper, soaking wet and heavy, kept pulling him back down. I then saw an arm cloaked by a white robe reach under his diaper and give him a boost up over the rocks. Very clearly, not in a dreamlike way, I heard these words: "Because you asked, his life was spared. My grace is sufficient for thee."

The vision became my inspiration for Dustin's two-year portrait, a "Heavenly Birthday Party." Every time I look at this special portrait, I am reminded of how blessed I am to still have him with me. I marvel over the mysteries of time, of angels and of premonitions, and how they all came together in prayer that day. I am aware of the awesome grace of God, and His power to intervene in our lives in amazing ways.

Lisa Jane

Show Your marvelous lovingkindness by Your right hand,

O You who save those who trust in You

From those who rise up against them.

Keep me as the apple of Your eye;

Hide me under the shadow of Your wings.

PSALM 17:7–8 NKJV

For I can do everything through Christ

who gives me strength.

PHILIPPIANS 4:13 NLT

He takes care of his people like a shepherd. He gathers them
like lambs in his arms and carries them close to him.
He gently leads the mothers of the lambs.

ISAIAH 40:11 NCV

The LORD is my shepherd; I shall not want.
He makes me to lie down in green pastures;
He leads me beside the still waters. He restores my soul...

PSALM 23:1–3 NKJV

When God has become our Shepherd, our Refuge,
our Fortress, then we can reach out to Him in the midst
of a broken world and feel at home while still on the way.

HENRI J. NOUWEN

*S*tress and hurt sometimes grab you by the throat and threaten to take away everything you've got. For some people, stress is a little different than for others. Some people's stress is wondering where to buy their next pair of $200 jeans because they aren't going to be as cool as the next person walking down the street. Some people's stress is hoping to make payments on their home and car and every bill, and to take care of their children in order to know they are safely off to school in the morning and home at the end of the day. Some people's stress is hoping to God they have enough money to buy food to ease hunger pangs for one more day, and hoping that some day they'll have enough money to be able to worry about paying a mortgage or having a car to drive their kids to school. Some people's stress is dealing with the fact that tons of water is bearing down on their homes and stores and streets because of a recent hurricane.

No matter what stress you are dealing with in your life, someone, somewhere is dealing with something greater, heavier, scarier than what you're dealing with, and it's better to just enjoy the moment because in a couple of minutes it may very well be gone.

*L*acy Pittman, a teenager wise beyond her years, wrote these insightful words the day she was killed in a car accident. Lacy's mother is the one who asked me to create this book for all who grieve the loss of a loved one.

IN LOVING MEMORY OF LACY PITTMAN
NOVEMBER 4, 1987 – SEPTEMBER 6, 2005

*N*ever lose an opportunity of seeing anything that is beautiful; for beauty is God's handwriting—a wayside sacrament. Welcome it in every fair face, in every fair sky, in every fair flower, and thank God for it as a cup of blessing.

RALPH WALDO EMERSON

*I*n old Chinese art, there is just one outstanding object, perhaps a flower. Everything else in the picture is subordinate. An integrated life is like that. What is that one flower? As I see it now, it is the will of God. I used to pray that God would do this or that. Now I pray that God will make His will known to me.

MADAM CHIANG KAI-SHEK

*F*or I am persuaded that neither death nor life, nor angels nor principalities nor powers, nor things present nor things to come, nor height nor depth, nor any other created thing, shall be able to separate us from the love of God which is in Christ Jesus our Lord.

ROMANS 8:38–39 NKJV

had once seen a photograph of a beautiful grieving angel, a statue at a local cemetery. Wanting to capture that magnificent image in photography, my assistant, Tessa, and I went there to seek her out. We only had an hour before we had to be back at the studio, but we found her just in time.

It was a cloudy day, and the outdoor light was really flat. But as we approached the angel statue, we saw a soft light gently begin to backlight her. Tessa looked at me, stunned, and said, "Do you see the light on her? Where it is coming from?" It was a mystery.

The angel's hand had broken off, so I reached up to a magnolia tree to pluck a flower for her, and a flower fell right into my hand! Another small miracle. I gave our angel the flower, laying it over her hand to soften the image. We only had about ten minutes to photograph her, and as soon as we finished we both noticed that her beautiful light was gone. We immediately left the cemetery, feeling strongly as though we had been part of a beautiful, spiritual experience.

Back at the studio, I started developing the images that we had taken of our angel, whom we had begun to call Grace. And when I saw what became my favorite shot of Grace, I started screaming, unable to contain myself. Within minutes, my entire staff had run into the room to see what was the matter.

Speechless, I could only point to the tiny angel, made solely by God, that appeared in the trees above Grace's head. I was so excited and moved that after twenty years of photographing angels I had finally been chosen to capture a real one! I could not wait to e-mail a copy of the image to one of my best friends, Rebecca, who is a very spiritual person and a photographer herself. I wasted no time sending her the picture of Grace and the amazing story behind it.

What I wasn't prepared for was Rebecca's reply. I had known that years earlier Rebecca and her grandmother had been in a terrible car accident. Her grandmother did not survive, and Rebecca could not escape the feeling that she was somehow at fault. Every year on the anniversary of the crash, she would pray for God to send her some sign that her grandmother did not blame her, that she was safe in His kingdom, and that the accident was part of a divine plan. I

didn't know that that day was the
anniversary of the terrible accident!
Also, her grandmother's last name
was Hill, and if you'll look closely
you'll see the name Hill engraved
at the bottom of the statue. Rebecca
also told me, being from Louisiana,
she always said her favorite flower
was the magnolia.

Rebecca was so relieved and
thankful that her grief could now
become acceptance and that her
heart could finally be at peace.
More importantly, she knew that
her grandmother was at peace as
well, shining her light and love on
Rebecca. God had spoken to her,
and I believe that if we'll open our
eyes and ears, we can all hear His
gentle whisper even in the darkest
times of our lives.

$\mathscr{G}$od will wipe away every tear from their eyes;

there shall be no more death,

nor sorrow, nor crying. There shall be no more pain,

for the former things have passed away.

REVELATION 21:4 NKJV

I waited patiently for the LORD. He turned to me and heard my cry. He lifted me out of the pit of destruction, out of the sticky mud. He stood me on a rock and made my feet steady. He put a new song in my mouth, a song of praise to our God. Many will see this and worship him. Then they will trust the LORD.

PSALM 40:1–3 NCV

*G*od comforts. He doesn't pity. He picks us up, dries our tears, soothes our fears, and lifts our thoughts beyond the hurt.

ROBERT SCHULLER

*B*elievers, look up—take courage. The angels are nearer than you think.

BILLY GRAHAM

Do you believe that God is near? He wants you to. He wants you
to know that He is in the midst of your world. Wherever you are as you read
these words, He is present. . . .And He is more than near. He is active.

MAX LUCADO

$\mathcal{B}$e merciful to me, O God,

be merciful to me!

For my soul trusts in You;

And in the shadow of Your wings

I will make my refuge,

Until these calamities have passed by.

I will cry out to God Most High,

To God who performs all things for me.

He shall send from heaven and save me...

Psalm 57:1–3 NKJV

Joy, joyful, joyous. These glad words make over 200 appearances through the Bible; one fourth of which occur in the Psalms. The psalmists sing, shout, and cry for joy. Their hearts leap for joy. They write of being anointed by the oil of joy and even speak of being clothed with joy! What brings us joy? Sports events, concerts, raises, shopping, and—according to the advertisements—an assortment of allergy-relief medications. The psalmists looked elsewhere for joy.

They found joy

> in God's salvation (Psalm 51:12)
>
> in God's guidance (Psalm 67:4)
>
> in God's name (Psalm 89:12)
>
> in God's unfailing love (Psalm 90:14)
>
> in God's comfort (Psalm 94:19)
>
> in God Himself (Psalm 43:4).

Today we find joy in events and things. The palmists found joy in a Person, the living God. Events are temporary. God is eternal! Therein lies the key to everlasting joy.

ALICIA BRITT CHOLE
PURE JOY

I find rest in God; only he gives me hope.

He is my rock and my salvation.

He is my defender; I will not be defeated.

My honor and salvation come from God.

He is my mighty rock and my protection.

PSALM 62:5–7 NCV

B ut the Lord is faithful, who will establish you

and guard you from the evil one.

And we have confidence in the Lord

concerning you, both that you do

and will do the things we command you.

Now may the Lord direct your hearts into the love

of God and into the patience of Christ.

2 THESSALONIANS 3:3–5 NKJV

The Difference Between Strength and Courage

It takes strength to be firm,
It takes courage to be gentle.

It takes strength to stand guard,
It takes courage to let it down.

It takes strength to conquer,
It takes courage to surrender.

It takes strength to be certain,
It takes courage to have doubt

It takes strength to fit in,
It takes courage to stand out.

It takes strength to feel a friend's pain,
It takes courage to feel your own pain.

It takes strength to hide your scars,
It takes courage to show them.

It takes strength to stand alone,
It takes courage to lean on another.

It takes strength to love,
It takes courage to be loved.

It takes strength to survive,
It takes courage to live.

DAVID GRIFFITH

My Lord,
You have heard the cry
of my heart
because it was You
who cried out within
my heart.

THOMAS MERTON

Remember, your life is not a dress rehearsal.
Savor this day as if it were your last. You cannot change
the past, and there are no guarantees for the future.

Lisa Jane

Therefore, since we are receiving a kingdom that cannot be shaken,
let us be thankful, and so worship God acceptably
with reverence and awe, for our "God is a consuming fire."

HEBREWS 12:28–29

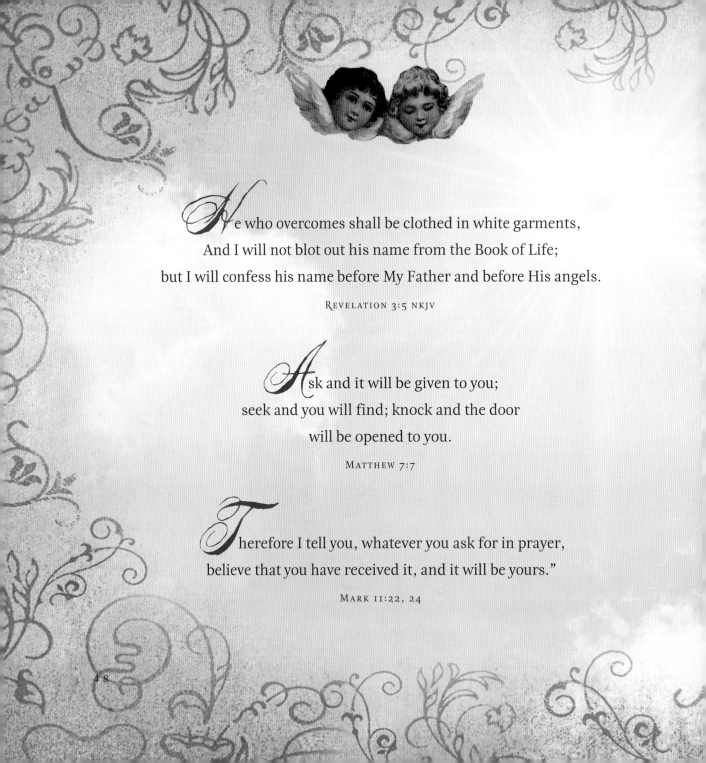

He who overcomes shall be clothed in white garments,

And I will not blot out his name from the Book of Life;

but I will confess his name before My Father and before His angels.

REVELATION 3:5 NKJV

Ask and it will be given to you;

seek and you will find; knock and the door

will be opened to you.

MATTHEW 7:7

Therefore I tell you, whatever you ask for in prayer,

believe that you have received it, and it will be yours."

MARK 11:22, 24

*In those times I can't seem to find God,
I rest in the assurance He knows how to find me.*

NEVA COYLE

*Come to me, all you who are weary
and burdened, and I will give you rest.
Take my yoke upon you and learn from me,
for I am gentle and humble in heart,
and you will find rest for your souls."*

MATTHEW 11:28–29

*Carry the cross patiently,
and with perfect submission;
and in the end it shall carry you.*

THOMAS A. KEMPIS

Lisa Janes

here two or three come together in my name, there I am with them.

MATTHEW 18:20

What is to give light must endure burning.

VIKTOR FRANKL

When you recognize God as Creator,
you will admire Him.
When you recognize His wisdom,
you will rely on Him.
But only when He saves you
will you worship Him.

MAX LUCADO

The LORD is my strength and my song;
he has become my salvation.
He is my God, and I will praise him,
my father's God, and I will exalt him.

EXODUS 15:2

*T*he path of the righteous
is like the first gleam of dawn,
shining ever brighter
till the full light of day.

PROVERBS 4:18

*T*he courage of life is often a less
dramatic spectacle than the
courage of a final moment
but is no less than a magnificent
mixture of triumph and tragedy.

JOHN FITZGERALD KENNEDY

55

$\mathcal{D}$o not pray for an easy life.

Pray to be a strong person.

NADIA COMANECI

*D*o not be anxious
about anything,
but in everything,
by prayer and petition,
with thanksgiving,
present your requests to God.
And the peace of God,
which transcends
all understanding,
will guard your hearts
and your minds
in Christ Jesus.

PHILIPPIANS 4:6–7

*T*he most difficult prayer, and the prayer which, therefore costs us
the most striving, is persevering prayer, the prayer which faints not,
but continues steadfastly until the answer comes.

O. HALLESBY

Let the light of your face

shine upon us, O LORD.

PSALM 4:6

Do not anticipate trouble or worry about what

may never happen. Keep in the sunlight.

BENJAMIN FRANKLIN

No man ever sank under the burden of the day. It is when

tomorrow's burden is added to the burden of today that

the weight is more than a man can bear. Never load yourself so.

If you find yourself so loaded, at least remember

this: it is your own doing, not God's. He begs you to leave

the future to Him, and mind the present.

GEORGE MacDONALD

60

*T*he LORD is my light
and my salvation—Whom shall I fear?
The LORD is the strength of my life—
Of whom shall I be afraid?

PSALM 27:1

*Y*our sun will never set again,
and your moon will wane no more;
the LORD will be your everlasting light,
and your days of sorrow will end.

ISAIAH 60:20

*D*on't be sad for me when I'm gone for I will have lived every day of my life
for that moment. And should you be at life's crossroads, faced with the painful
and uncertain possibilities of that moment, be comforted with joy and rejoice
because in knowing Him, either way you Win!

DENA JOY DAVIDSON

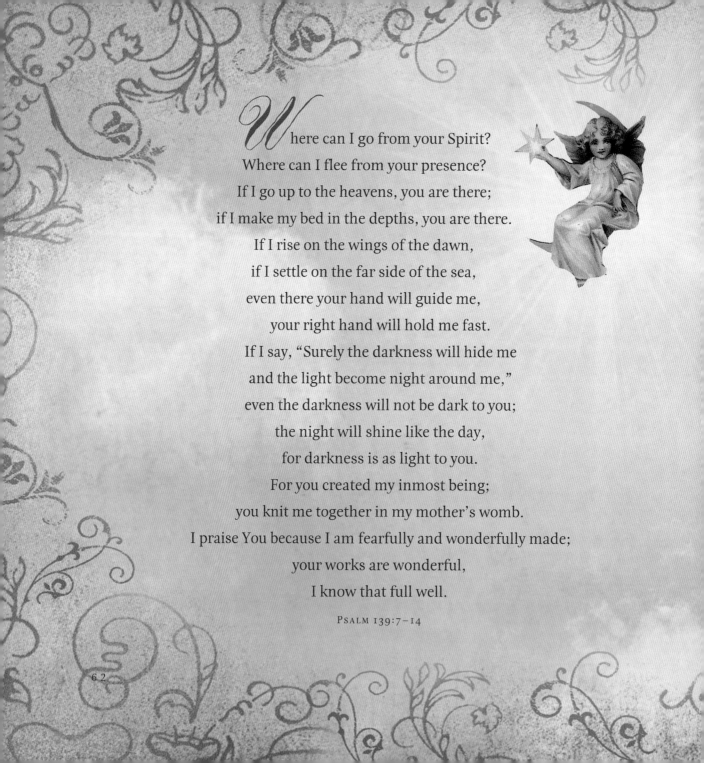

Where can I go from your Spirit?
Where can I flee from your presence?
If I go up to the heavens, you are there;
if I make my bed in the depths, you are there.
If I rise on the wings of the dawn,
if I settle on the far side of the sea,
even there your hand will guide me,
your right hand will hold me fast.
If I say, "Surely the darkness will hide me
and the light become night around me,"
even the darkness will not be dark to you;
the night will shine like the day,
for darkness is as light to you.
For you created my inmost being;
you knit me together in my mother's womb.
I praise You because I am fearfully and wonderfully made;
your works are wonderful,
I know that full well.

PSALM 139:7–14

*I*f joy were the only emotion God intended us to feel, He could just zap us and take us to heaven right now. . . .The truth is that our trials are a furnace forging us into gold.

BARBARA JOHNSON

When you pass through the waters,

I will be with you;

and when you pass through the rivers,

they will not sweep over you.

When you walk through the fire,

you will not be burned;

the flames will not set you ablaze.

ISAIAH 43:2

Whatever the circumstances, whatever the call,

whatever the duty, whatever the price, whatever the sacrifice—

His strength will be your strength in your hour of need.

BILLY GRAHAM

We all have a choice in how we respond to pain. We can become angry, bitter, or controlling. We can choose the denial route or we can choose to grow. Dealing with pain is a process, and as long as we realize God is bigger than the pain, we can live with hope that at some point we will be on the other side of it. When life is overwhelmingly difficult, I've chosen not to waste the pain but instead, to use it to learn everything I can about the heart and character of God. In doing so I have tasted His transforming grace.

*C*all upon me in the day
of trouble; I will deliver you,
and you will honor me.

PSALM 50:15

*F*or I will not trust in my bow,

neither shall my sword save me.

But Thou hast saved us from our enemies,

And hast put them to shame that hated us.

In God we boast all the day long,

and praise thy name for ever. Selah.

PSALM 44:6–8 KJV

*Y*ou will break the bow if you
keep it always bent.

GREEK PROVERB

*S*hout for joy to the LORD, all the earth,
burst into jubilant song with music,
make music to the LORD with the harp,
with the harp and the sound of singing,
with trumpets and the blast of the ram's horn—
shout for joy before the LORD, the King.

PSALM 98:4-6

*W*hen the soul is full of peace and joy,
outward surroundings and circumstances
are of comparatively little account.

HANNAH WHITALL SMITH

*I*f God had wanted me otherwise,
He would have created me otherwise.

JOHANN WOLFGANG VON GOETHE

*B*e cheerful no matter what; pray all the time; thank God
no matter what happens. This is the way God
wants you who belong to Christ Jesus to live.

1 THESSALONIANS 5:16–18 MSG

*T*he ultimate measure of a man is not where he stands
in moments of comfort and convenience, but where he
stands at times of challenge and controversy.

MARTIN LUTHER KING, JR.

73

Lisa Jane

*G*od may be invisible, but He's in touch. You may not be able to see Him, but He is in control. . . .That includes all of life—past, present, future.

CHARLES SWINDOLL

Just thinking about angels can give us a fresh reminder that there's another world besides this one that clings so closely all around us.

DAVID JEREMIAH

$\mathcal{W}$e are all made to reach out beyond our grasp.

Oswald Chambers

$\mathcal{A}$n Angel of Paradise, no less,
is always beside me, wrapped in
everlasting ecstasy on his Lord.
so I am ever under the gaze of an Angel
who protects and prays for me.

Pope John XXIII

To everything there is a season,
A time for every purpose under heaven:

A time to be born, And a time to die;

A time to plant, And a time to pluck what is planted;

A time to kill, And a time to heal;

A time to break down, And a time to build up;

A time to weep, And a time to laugh;

A time to mourn, And a time to dance;

A time to cast away stones, And a time to gather stones;

A time to embrace, And a time to refrain from embracing;

A time to gain, And a time to lose;

A time to keep, And a time to throw away;

A time to tear, And a time to sew;

A time to keep silence, And a time to speak;

A time to love, And a time to hate,

A time of war, And a time of peace.

ECCLESIASTES 3:1–8 NKJV

After Hurricane Katrina destroyed their New Orleans homes, many families with children relocated to Houston, where I live. Because I am blessed with so many generous clients with children, my studio became a collection and distribution center for clothes, shoes, and toys for the hurricane refugees. We were able to give away everything we had collected—except one large, bright pink shopping bag overflowing with the most beautiful collection of girls' shoes imaginable. Every little girl who visited went straight for the pink bag, but none of them were able to squeeze their feet into the tiny shoes. My assistant and I decided to pray for God to send the perfect child for the rainbow collection of shoes, someone who was in need, someone who would appreciate them.

The next afternoon, I was photographing a single mother and her three daughters for a Web page that she was creating for her ministry. (You can take a peek at www.inmothersarms.org.) The mother had AIDS. What she wanted most, besides to take care of her own three girls, was to embrace and empower other children affected by HIV and AIDS.

Near the end of the session, I noticed the shoes her middle daughter was wearing, a very worn-out pair of tennis shoes, probably hand-me-downs. Just as I was asking the girl what size shoe she wore, my assistant opened the door to check on the session and heard her mother reply, "A size six." I saw my assistant's face light up, and off she ran for the coveted pink bag.

After the session was over, I handed the bag to her and whispered, "I think God wanted you to have these shoes." She carefully took the bag and peeked inside. Her eyes widened. She glanced up at her mom, burst into tears of joy, and ran out of the room, clutching the treasured bag as if it were her lifeline. Her mom was trying so hard to hold back her tears that she couldn't speak, but the next day she called me and shared her story.

The day before the portrait session, the girls were organizing their clothes, and her daughter realized that she only had the battered old tennis shoes to wear.

She begged her mom to buy her a pair of flip-flops so she wouldn't be embarrassed, and her mother told her that she was really sorry, but they just could not afford any new shoes. But, she said, they served a big God who was capable of anything, and He could supply all of their needs. So they prayed that He would provide her with a pair of flip-flops.

Now the little girl was the recipient of that precious pink bag, filled to the top with beautiful new flip-flops, dress shoes, and tennis shoes. She'd received an abundant answer to her honest, heartfelt prayer.

Never underestimate the power of prayer, the grace of God, or a little girl's newfound faith.

Lisa Jane

Lisa Jane

*or God was pleased to have
all his fullness dwell in him.*

COLOSSIANS 1:19

t seems today that everywhere we turn people are talking about spirituality. People are recognizing that there is power and life beyond what we can touch and see and hear. So they search this way and that, in outer space or in the inner space of their hearts—trying to connect with something that gives them purpose and meaning.

Lloyd Ogilvie, the chaplain of the U.S. Senate, made a profound statement in a commencement address: "God has revealed Himself in the natural world and throughout history, but sublimely in Jesus Christ. He has opened His heart and revealed his unchanging, unqualified, unlimited love in the grace of the Lord Jesus." Beautiful. That's the real spiritual message.

PAUL FAULKNER

*T*he guardian Angels of Life sometimes fly so high as to be
beyond our sight, but they are always looking down upon us.

JEAN PAULKISHTER

*M*y home is in heaven.
I'm just traveling through this world.

BILLY GRAHAM

*I*f you live for the next world, you get this one in the deal;
but if you live only for this world, you lose them both.

C.S. LEWIS

85

Lisa Jane

*N*ot only so, but we also rejoice in our sufferings, because we know that suffering produces perseverance; perseverance, character; and character, hope. And hope does not disappoint us, because God has poured out His love into our hearts by the Holy Spirit, whom he has given us.

ROMANS 5:3–5

*T*hen you will call, and the LORD will answer; you will cry for help, and he will say: Here am I.

ISAIAH 58:9

In the shadow of his hand he hid me;
he made me into a polished arrow
and concealed me in his quiver.

ISAIAH 49:2

The God of all grace, who called you to his
eternal glory in Christ, after you have suffered a little
while, will himself restore you and make you
strong, firm and steadfast.

1 PETER 5:10

The greatness comes not when things go always good for you.
But the greatness comes when you're really tested, when you
take some knocks, some disappointments, when sadness
comes. Because only if you've been in the deepest valley
can you ever know how magnificent it is
to be on the highest mountain.

RICHARD NIXON

Lisa Jane

*T*he eyes of the LORD are on those who fear him,

on those whose hope is in his unfailing love. . . .

We wait in hope for the LORD; he is our help and our shield.

In him our hearts rejoice, for we trust in his holy name.

May your unfailing love rest upon us, O LORD,

even as we put our hope in you.

PSALM 33:18, 20–22

*E*veryone has a unique role to fill
in the world and is important in some
respect. Everyone, including and perhaps
especially you, is indispensable.

NATHANIEL HAWTHORNE

92

*G*od stirs up our comfortable nests, and pushes us
over the edge of them, and we are forced to use our wings
to save ourselves from fatal falling. Read your trials
in this light, and see if your wings are being developed.

HANNAH WHITALL SMITH

*H*ow priceless is your unfailing love!
Both high and low among men
find refuge in the shadow of Your wings.

PSALM 36:7

*D*o not worry about your life, what you will eat or drink;
or about your body, what you will wear...Look at the birds of the air;
they do not sow or reap or store away in barns, and yet your
heavenly Father feeds them. Are you not much more valuable
than they? Who of you by worrying can add a
single hour to his life? So do not worry..."

MATTHEW 6:25–27, 31

A Prayer for Protection

The light of God surrounds me,
The love of God enfolds me,
The power of God protects me;
The presence of God watches over me.
Wherever I am God is, and all is well.

JAMES FREEMAN

If suffering went out of life,
courage, tenderness, pity, faith, patience,
and love in its divinity would go out of life, too.

FATHER ANDREW

Lisa Jane

Sisters don't need words—
they listen with their hearts.
They are earthly angels sent to comfort and
minister to you through the trials
of life, and help you fulfill your dreams.
I cherish my sisters.

Lisa Jane

Two are better than one,
Because they have a good reward
for their labor. For if they fall,
one will lift up his companion.
But woe to him who is alone when he falls,
for he has no one to help him up.

ECCLESIASTES 4:9–10

Lisa Jane

God is our refuge and strength, A very present help in trouble.
Therefore we will not fear, Even though the earth be removed,
And though the mountains be carried into the midst of the sea. . . .
The LORD of hosts is with us; The God of Jacob is our refuge. Selah.

PSALM 46:1–2, 7

You gain strength, courage, and confidence
by every experience in which you really stop
to look fear in the face. You are able to say
to yourself, "I lived through this horror,
I can take the next thing that comes along.". . .
You must do the thing you think you cannot do.

ELEANOR ROOSEVELT

My comfort in my suffering is this:
Your promise preserves my life.
May your unfailing love be my comfort,
according to your promise to your servant.

PSALM 119:50, 76

In this life we will encounter hurts and trials that we will not be able
to change; we are just going to have to allow them to change us.

RON LEE DAVIS

All this trying leads up to the vital moment at which
you turn to God and say, "You must do this. I can't."

C. S. LEWIS

When the train goes through a tunnel and the
world gets dark, do you jump out? Of course not.
You sit still and trust the engineer to get you through.

CORRIE TEN BOOM

This is my prayer for you:
that your love will grow more and more;
that you will have knowledge and understanding
with your love; that you will see the difference
between good and bad and will choose the good;
that you will be pure and without wrong
for the coming of Christ; that you
will be filled with the good things
produced in your life by Christ
to bring glory and praise to God.

PHILIPPIANS 1:9–11 NCV

Lisa Jane

*B*ecause Your lovingkindness is better than life,

My lips shall praise You. Thus I will bless You while I live;

I will lift up my hands in Your name.

My soul shall be satisfied as with marrow and fatness,

And my mouth shall praise You with joyful lips.

When I remember You on my bed, I meditate on You

in the night watches. Because You have been my help,

There fore in the shadow of Your wings I will rejoice.

PSALM 63:3–7 NKJV

I will praise you, LORD, with all my heart.

I will tell all the miracles you have done.

I will be happy because of you;

God Most High, I will sing praises to your name.

PSALM 9:1–2 NCV

*L*ook to the LORD and his strength; seek his face always.
Remember the wonders he has done, his miracles,
and the judgments he pronounced.

1 CHRONICLES 16:11–12

*L*ive your life while you have it. Life is a
splendid gift—there is nothing small about it.

FLORENCE NIGHTINGALE

*T*he Spirit of the Sovereign LORD is on me, because the LORD
has anointed me to preach good news to the poor.
He has sent me to bind up the brokenhearted, . . .
to comfort all who mourn, and provide
for those who grieve in Zion—to bestow
on them a crown of beauty instead of ashes,
the oil of gladness instead of mourning,
and a garment of praise instead of a spirit of despair.

ISAIAH 61:1–3

Lisa Jane

Darkness cannot put out the Light.
It can only make God brighter.

AUTHOR UNKNOWN

Send forth your light and your truth,
let them guide me; let them bring me
to your holy mountain,
to the place where you dwell.
Then will I go to the altar of God,
to God, my joy and my delight.
I will praise you with the harp,
O God, my God.

PSALM 43:3–4

The refiner is never very far from the mouth
of the furnace when his gold is in the fire.

CHARLES SPURGEON

Lisa Jane

*H*e will command his angels concerning you to guard you in all your ways.

PSALM 91:11

*A*ngels speak. They appear and reappear.
They feel with an apt sense of emotion.
While angels may become visible by choice,
our eyes are not conducted to see them ordinarily
any more than we can see the dimensions
of a nuclear field, the structure of atoms, or the
electricity that flows through copper wiring.

BILLY GRAHAM

*T*he angels are near to us. [They] have long arms, and,
although they stand before the face and in the presence of God
and his son Christ, they are hard by and about us in those
affairs which by God we are commanded to take in hand.

MARTIN LUTHER

109

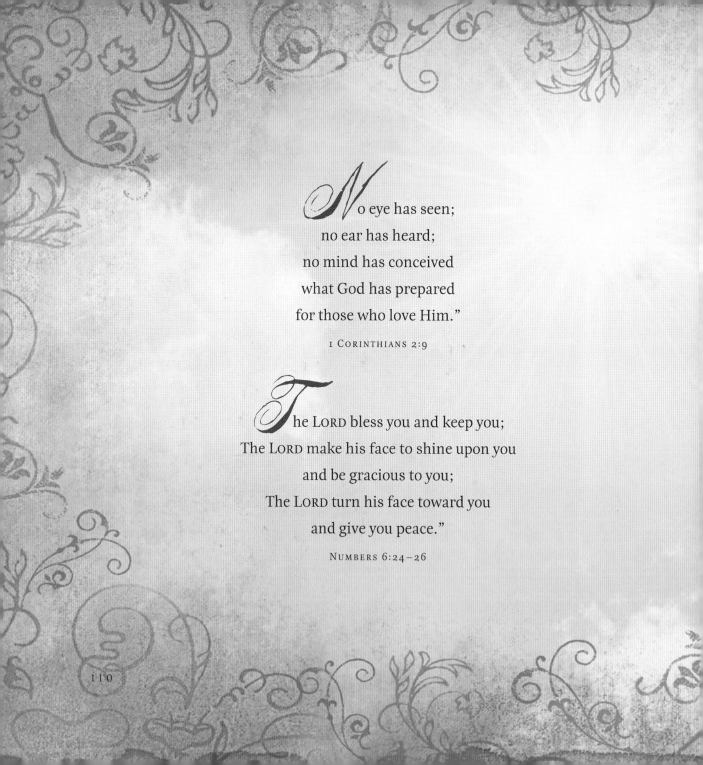

*N*o eye has seen;
no ear has heard;
no mind has conceived
what God has prepared
for those who love Him."

1 CORINTHIANS 2:9

*T*he LORD bless you and keep you;
The LORD make his face to shine upon you
and be gracious to you;
The LORD turn his face toward you
and give you peace."

NUMBERS 6:24–26

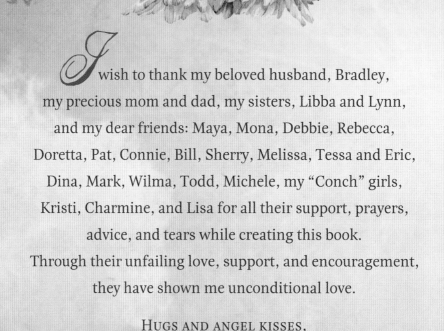

I wish to thank my beloved husband, Bradley,
my precious mom and dad, my sisters, Libba and Lynn,
and my dear friends: Maya, Mona, Debbie, Rebecca,
Doretta, Pat, Connie, Bill, Sherry, Melissa, Tessa and Eric,
Dina, Mark, Wilma, Todd, Michele, my "Conch" girls,
Kristi, Charmine, and Lisa for all their support, prayers,
advice, and tears while creating this book.
Through their unfailing love, support, and encouragement,
they have shown me unconditional love.

HUGS AND ANGEL KISSES,
XOXO,

Lisa Jane

*W*hen I stand before God at the end of my life, I would hope
that I would not have a single bit of talent left, and could say,
"I used everything you gave me."

ERMA BOMBECK